Heidegger, Habermas and the Mobile Phone

George Myerson

Series editor: Richard Appignanesi

ICON BOOKS UK

TOTEM BOOKS USA

Published in the UK in 2001
by Icon Books Ltd., Grange Road,
Duxford, Cambridge CB2 4QF
E-mail: info@iconbooks.co.uk
www.iconbooks.co.uk

Published in the USA in 2001
by Totem Books
Inquiries to: Icon Books Ltd.,
Grange Road, Duxford,
Cambridge CB2 4QF, UK

Sold in the UK, Europe, South Africa
and Asia by Faber and Faber Ltd.,
3 Queen Square, London WC1N 3AU
or their agents

Distributed to the trade in the USA by
National Book Network Inc.,
4720 Boston Way, Lanham,
Maryland 20706

Distributed in the UK, Europe,
South Africa and Asia by
Macmillan Distribution Ltd.,
Houndmills, Basingstoke RG21 6XS

Distributed in Canada by
Penguin Books Canada,
10 Alcorn Avenue, Suite 300,
Toronto, Ontario M4V 3B2

Published in Australia in 2001
by Allen & Unwin Pty. Ltd.,
83 Alexander Street,
Crows Nest, NSW 2065

Library of Congress catalog
card number applied for

Text copyright © 2001 George Myerson

Series editor: Richard Appignanesi

ISBN 1 84046 236 1

Typesetting by Wayzgoose

Printed and bound in the UK by
Cox & Wyman Ltd., Reading

'It Was Good To Talk': Mobile Phones and German Philosophers

'If you want to keep pace with the changing environment . . . the global economy of the day, you need a fast means of communications,' says Tansa Musa.

'Front Page World', www.bbc.news.co.uk,
4 September 2000

The BBC has just asked a citizen of Cameroon to explain what it calls 'mobile phone frenzy' which is 'hitting' the country. The answer is twofold. Mobiles are practical, they have their uses. But beyond the practicality, the mobile is the object which most closely embodies the spirit of the 'changing environment'. If you want to assure yourself that you belong to the new century, this is the object to have in your hands – unless it's a 'hands-free'. Musa's brilliantly concise response points towards a big question: *how* has the once anodyne 'telephone' become the new must-have mobile?

At the moment, as the new millennium starts, we are witnessing, and being addressed by, a ubiquitous campaign to promote the mobile phone. This mobile propaganda is extraordinary in its energy, its resources and its cultural impact. There are the old-style ads, but there is also a torrent of information released through diverse media, on the web, via other products and sales outlets. You can hardly tune in to a major sporting event without finding the logo of a mobile company featured either among the competitors or over the occasion as a whole.

The promotion is twofold: its subject is first of all a whole new technology, and then an individual brand. This doubleness must pose interesting dilemmas for publicists of the individual corporations: can you promote your brand specifically or are you really just promoting the whole technology? There is plenty to say about the mobile campaign. You can deconstruct the images, as with all such publicity. You can find stereotypes and ideological undercurrents. But in this 'Postmodern Encounter', I propose to look at this mobile hubbub from a more surprising perspective: an alien perspective.

Our encounter will be between this new mobile culture and two leading thinkers of the 20th century: Martin Heidegger and Jürgen Habermas. (See 'Appendix' for brief profiles.) In his great work, *Being and Time* (1927), Heidegger initiated one of the most important 20th-century discussions of talk or, as he also called it, 'discourse'. These ideas were taken up, criticised and developed in different ways by many European and American thinkers, notably among German philosophers of communication, of whom the latest representative is Jürgen Habermas, whose *Theory of Communicative Action* (1981) has shaped two decades of debate about dialogue and modern society. The nub of this encounter is the idea of communication itself, for, in their different ways, both the 20th-century philosophers and the 21st-century mobile persuaders claim to be redefining what it means for human beings to communicate.

What makes this encounter a postmodern one? In architecture especially, 'postmodern' often means the mixing of old and new, futuristic and archaic styles. This encounter is postmodern in that architectural sense: here the old thinkers come together with the new cultural wizards. Apart from striking sparks off one another, these contrasting perspectives also reveal – as they collide – something significant about the break between the old and the new centuries. Both the philosophers and the mobile campaigners are interested not just in routine communication, but in the road to utopia. For all their differences, the two 'discourses' share the view that modern utopia will be about ideal communication.

The 'Great Mobilisation' of the Year 2000: 'It's great to communicate.'

'Well, my friends, think of the old Che Guevara poster you once had on your bedroom wall. This is a popular uprising, carried out by mobile phone ...'
Leandra de Lisle, 'My friends on the barricades', www.guardianunlimited.co.uk, 13 September 2000

How many meanings this new telephone can carry! Symbol of the new global economy one minute, the very next minute the mobile is an emblem of the new revolution. It seems as if this magic thing can release the hidden power latent in the ordinary process of communication. By the magic of the mobile, a few truck drivers and farmers are trans-formed into a 'petrol blockade' of Britain to rival the Second World War. Even in such news items, the march of the mobile campaign goes on, fuelled – unlike everything else – by protest and picketing as much as by Internet and e-commerce.

Anything as massive as the mobile campaign most

certainly deserves its own name, and clips like this glimpse of the new 'barricades' suggest one: MOBILISATION. Alongside its martial connotations, the word also has useful echoes of 'globalisation', the catchphrase of the new century. Mobilisation is a way of connecting what Tansa Musa in Cameroon says about the new telephone in the 'global economy' and what Leandra de Lisle writes about the new outlaws and their modern-day smoke-signals. What is being 'mobilised' in all the imagery and persuasion, the catchphrasing and informing? In the first place, however obvious it might sound, what is occurring is the mobilisation of that old telephone. The mobilisation of the phone isn't really a technological process – it's cultural. The problem isn't to *invent* a machine, but to get us all to *adopt* it, to feel we need it. Because, of course, it's we that need to be mobilised.

Let's look briefly at the ingredients of mobilisation. The classic British Telecom telephone slogan of the last century was: 'It's good to talk . . .'. That is really a pre-mobilisation slogan. Something radical has happened since that now nostalgic time. Talk is still an important theme in the massive cultural text that is being woven around the mobile. But, especially in the more 'informative' presentations, you have dizzying images of talking all around, a feeling that does perhaps match our everyday experience of the onset of the mobile era. Instead of the old-style 'conversation', you have the multiplication of talk:

[T]*he number of cellular phones in this country* [is estimated] *to be near 77 million, with more than 37,500 people signing up for wireless phone service each day.* **And these users are talking more than ever before.** . . . [T]*here is too much traffic on the phone network* . . . [My emphasis.]

New York Times, 19 August 2000

In this clip, you find the key ingredients of the new mobilisation. First come the numbers; the new promotion of the mobile is all about numbers – and they are staggering. So many people are signing up per second, so many people will be on the mobile by next week, next month, next year. Second, there is the sense of what James Gleick calls 'acceleration'. You could no longer say that 'it's good to talk'; the message is much more zappy, more like: 'It's great to communicate!'

[handwritten margin note: mobilisation = numbers + acceleration]

8

The old familiar telephone has become part of something else, *that* is the message, and in the process there has been an explosion of energy, an immense interconnection. Old slow-moving 'talk' is being rapidly pushed aside by its faster cousin 'communication'. You can feel that pressure in the little warning note: all that talk is making the traffic move too slowly, a kind of communicative gridlock is setting in. We will need, the implication is, some better way to communicate in the future. The destiny of the mobile is to take us beyond the 'world of talk', into some other world where 'communication' means something far richer and also far quicker.

The phone is an object and a technology. But it is also part of a system of ideas, even a way of looking at everyday life. The phone has become part of an idea of the family, of intimacy, emergency and work. The message of mobilisation is that the old phone is no more, and so that old system of ideas has also passed away. You may assume that you know what a phone is and does, what it is for. But the essence of the language of mobile promotion is to show that you don't yet understand your phone. You are stuck in the last century, until you have 'got' mobilisation.

Talk is the starting point in understanding this new-style object, but soon the talking stops:

*It's perfectly **suited to talking to people**, to receiving short messages, screening short movie clips, holding video conferences on the move, receiving headlines.* [My emphasis.]

Orange Press Release, 13 July 2000

Yes, of course the mobile is about talking, but already they have to add 'to people' – an important phrase. You can no longer assume that people are on the receiving end of this 'talk'. Now talk is part of a web of uses – and here the phone is being redefined, and with it human communication. Again, there is a tremendous sense of multiplication, this time the multiplication of *functions* of your phone. Yes, it's good to talk, but look at all the other ways of communicating down the line.

And so there arises the possibility of this new advice:

*The Person You Are With is the **Most Important Person To Talk To**.* [My emphasis.]

Nokia Press Release, 12 July 2000

You can see here just how far talk itself is being re-made and even overtaken in the project of the mobile phone as it enters the 21st century. 'Talk' stands for an old sense of person-to-person presence and contact. The new phone mobilisers show you they aren't against such traditions, on the contrary. At the same time, you can see how this old sense of contact is being surrounded, new meanings pushing it aside. In Nokia's etiquette, there is a vivid picture of what the world must be like, before such advice is needed. The 'You' of this exhortation is being besieged by other voices, by rival message systems.

The philosopher Heidegger might well have agreed with Nokia about their general principle. He devoted a lot of time to the idea of 'being-with', and he certainly saw talking as part of our way to be with others. For Heidegger, in 1927, it was in such moments of contact that a way to be human emerged: 'Man shows himself as the entity which talks.'[1]

Heidegger meant even more than that it was just 'good to talk'. In his philosophy, the message was more like: 'It's human to talk.' For Heidegger, talking was the fundamental activity by which people expressed their experience of 'being-with' each

"It's human to talk."

11

other. From Heidegger's perspective, Nokia's principle is a basic truth, but there is something alarming about the need to remind everyone about it.

That preliminary encounter between Nokia and Heidegger suggests both an overlap and an antithesis. You could say that this is the development which the old philosophers 'asked for', when they made such a to-do about talk and communication! Are we on the threshold of the age when the essential vision of the communication-philosophy is going to become part of our everyday living? Or is the new age going to take 'communication' into territories undreamt of in the last century?

The Age of Communication: Universal Contact

One of the central statements of German communication philosophy was made by the philosopher Karl Jaspers soon after Heidegger had presented his ideas about being human: '[P]hilosophic truth sees all human beings as possible others with whom it remains our task to communicate.'[2]

Jaspers was writing in 1932, on the eve of Hitler; unlike Heidegger, he was a consistent anti-fascist. Taking off, nevertheless, from Heidegger's ideas about talking and being, he gives an extraordinary vision of the human condition. For Jaspers, it is our duty as human beings to communicate with all the others. There is no way of fulfilling this duty, and no way of compromising on it. If you think you possess the truth, then you can't stop short in the task of communication. In fact, if you take your ideas and beliefs at all seriously, then this is your duty. The idea follows directly from Heidegger on talking and being human, but it has a more obviously progressive spin.

So, one might say, has not the time of this universal communication at last arrived? Poor old Jaspers in 1932, what means of communication did he have at his limited disposal? Pens, type, print, and the old immobile phone. You'd be lucky to communicate with a few thousand people in such a pre-modern condition. If only he could have tuned in to the Nokia website, might he not have found much-needed encouragement to think that his task might be fulfilled in the future? Surely now, humanity can at last achieve what the old philosophers desired, and 'be-with' itself across the globe?

Here is a selection from the Nokia Press Releases Archive for January–July 2000:

10 February: new network to Thailand

3 March: new technology for Japan telecom

29 March: new technology for US apartments

4 April: network in Poland

5 April: technology trial in Hong Kong

12 April: new award in New Zealand

12 April: new networks in Germany

5 May: new joint factory opened by Hungarian and
  Finnish leaders

8 May: partnership in Israel

11 May: WAP to UK

11 May: advanced trials in Australia

15 May: network advance for Maroc telecom

18 May: commercial network in Norway

22 May: networks in Taiwan

26 May: network to Bolivia

6 June: new digital terminal for Asian market

8 June: WAP solution for Ukraine

14 June: new system in Greece

16 June: WAP networks in China

26 June: network for Finland

26 June: trials in Singapore of new technology

5 July: equipment to Estonia

5 July: network in Denmark

7 July: new data call in Philippines

10 July: network for Austria
11 July: broadband access in France
14 July: 'supply solution' in Belgium

This kind of list is at the core of mobilisation, with its sense of scale and accelerated pace. This archive proclaims the coming of the age when 'mobilisation' will take over from 'globalisation' as the motto on the flag. Now 'all human beings' truly are 'possible others' and we really can, it seems, undertake our moral 'task' and 'communicate with' them, every one of them.

Network after network: you can almost *see* the globe being encircled in a fine mesh of little connecting links. In the mobile vista, communication is on the verge of becoming truly a universal. One could call the outlook 'universal communication', and it is the philosophy implicit in mobilisation as a whole. Of course, such a philosophy fits in with other developments in our time, economic developments that have gone under the heading of 'globalisation'. But it still all sounds like the triumph of the communicative principle, as envisaged by Jaspers and Heidegger in the 1920s and 30s.

It may sound odd to credit mobile phone promotion with a philosophy. Yet this is more than an ordinary, familiar marketing campaign, though it is that as well, of course. The vision runs across official reports and expert statements, as well as ads and one-liners. Highlights across diverse media and institutions show the outlook unfolding. Here it is in 'bureaucrat-ese':

1.1 Their use has escalated over the past decade and to many they are now an essential part of business, commerce and society. Over the Christmas 1999 period alone approximately 4 million phones were sold in the UK and at present (April 2000) there are about 25 million mobile phones in circulation. This is equivalent to nearly one phone for every two people.

'The Stewart Report', independent expert group on
mobile phones, May 2000

Staid it may sound, but there is the same communication euphoria as on the commercial websites, the same sense of acceleration, and universality in the wings. This is how humanity is going to find itself, in the new era. Here is the British broadsheet press. In its electronic form, the vision is as follows:

Evidence of Britain's insatiable appetite for mobile phone technology emerged yesterday as figures showed that more than half the population has a mobile. The latest quarterly results showed that network operators had more than 30 million subscribers.

'Half of Britain on the Mobile',
www.guardianunlimited.co.uk, 6 July 2000

The key phrase here is 'more than half the population': what happened to the others? It is as if they had failed to register their presence in the world. Next the televised version:

It is believed 3.5 million people bought mobile phones between April and June – an 85% increase on the same period last year.

www.ITN.co.uk, 17 July 2000

And here it is in the US heavyweight press:

According to the ARC Group, a London consulting firm, about 100 million of the world's 500 million mobile phones in use by year-end will be capable of Internet access. Within three years, ARC says, an estimated 300 million of 900 million wireless phones will be Internet ready. Other industry forecasts say that in five years, as many as 500 million people worldwide – one of every dozen – will have phones or other devices capable of wireless Internet access.

New York Times, 10 July 2000

This last highlight adds many of the other key ingredients that make mobilisation distinct and different: it's not just people that are becoming interconnected, but technologies, systems. Surely, when you multiply the web by the mobile, you get universal interconnection? And is not this the destiny of communication, as anticipated by those old German philosophers?

For all the tempting links, the German philosophers would probably not endorse 'mobilisation', even though the two do have in common an immense emphasis on communication as *the* human activity. In the remaining sections, we shall look at the key ingredients in the mobile view of communication, and compare them with their philosophical equivalents. The result is a genuine 'close encounter', and also a striking cultural contrast.

What is 'Communication'? I and We

[T]*he whole concept of communication is being changed.*

Orange Press Release, 13 July 2000

First, let us take the mobilising of communication. Here we begin with the premise that does link the mobile campaign to modern philosophy: communication is a *concept*. There are different versions of this concept, and the mobile campaign is based on the idea that it is possible to change the whole meaning of communication itself. But what is the new concept of communication being adopted and endorsed by the mobile campaign?

Today, wireless phones provide more than 94 million, or one in every three people in the US, with the freedom to communicate – whenever they want, wherever they want.

Nokia Press Release, 12 July 2000

There are two key ideas: first, the sheer scale of interconnection; and second, by contrast, an idea of individual freedom. To be able to communicate is a basic aspect of being free. Indeed, the fact of communication is a key sign of being free. The whole tone of the distinctive mobile concept, however, is established by the recurrent 'they want'. In its mobilised version, communication is all about the fulfilment of an individual *desire* – a want. Being free to communicate is an aspect of getting what you want as much as possible.

There is another way of putting this, which involves ideas other than freedom:

[The new mobilised technology] *should help you take control of the way you communicate . . .*

'The Orange Way', www.orange.co.uk,
18 July 2000

At heart, the mobile concept is about being in control – as a separate and distinct individual. This is the basis of mobilising the concept of communication – that it's an activity undertaken by an individual, over which that individual seeks control. Being in control of communication means being the master of technology itself:

[The new phone-device] *becomes literally your personal communications centre ...*

Orange Press Release, 13 July 2000

The really striking idea is 'personal . . . centre'. This is a fundamental principle of the mobilisation of communication: *Communication is, at heart, a solitary action.* You have your own communications centre. So we arrive at a major bit of advice, embodying the basic practice of mobilisation. *Communication works best when there is only one person involved:*

[I]*t's cheaper than a phone call and doesn't require real-time availability of the two persons communicating, it's asynchronous ...*

New York Times, 14 March 2000

A postmodern paradox! On the one hand, we have a language of scale; on the other hand, we have the separate individual seeking goals. This paradox creates the atmosphere of mobilisation. Countless – but counted – individuals are seeking their desires separately, and yet unknowingly they are caught up in a huge system.

Now turn to the slow world of the German philosophers as *they* try to redefine the concept of communication. The contrast is touching, even heart-rending. This is Heidegger:

*Discourse which expresses itself is **communication**. Its tendency of Being is aimed at **bringing the hearer to participate in disclosed Being towards what is talked about** in the discourse.*[3]

The argument moves so slowly over the ground, trying to pin down the concept of communication which now moves so quickly. 'Communication' starts from 'discourse', from the language itself, endowed with a life of its own. This language seeks to be expressed, and when people give expression to it, then you have true communication. Heidegger's thinking is, therefore, right at the other extreme from the mobilised view. In Heidegger's approach, you could not look at communication in terms of an individual speaker wanting control. If there is a key individual in his definition, it's the hearer, not the speaker at all. Communication is all about the hearer's understanding. And what Heidegger means is that the hearer should have an experience of the subject being discussed which amounts to a sharing with the speaker. So to try to take control would be a violation of the whole nature of true communication. And the idea of a personal communications centre would be entirely self-contradictory! So too would the emphasis on massive numbers: communication has this personal contact at its heart.

Heidegger's idea evolves into Habermas's concept of 'communicative action'. Here too, there is a contrast with mobilised communication. You can't see communicative action as one person fulfilling an intention. The key to true communication, for Habermas, is 'understanding'. His communicative action is *the use of language with an orientation to reaching understanding*. Communicative action is shared action:

Reaching understanding is considered to be a process of reaching agreement among speaking and acting subjects.[4]

You only have this communication when there is a process by which people come to an understanding about something. And Habermas works out a contrast with what he calls 'instrumental' action or strategy, which is all about taking personal control and fulfilling personal goals.

Orientation to Success versus Orientation to reaching Understanding . . . [I]dentifying strategic and communicative action as types.[5]

If mobilisation were completed, the prime example of communication would not be *two people* – it would be *one* person, set in the context of millions of other separate people. Not that two-person contact would be denied, but it would be secondary. Whereas in the philosopher's tradition, the prime idea has to be two-person contact – or small group engagement.

So the issue isn't whether such a philosopher could or should use a mobile – why not? What's at stake is how to define the *act* of communication itself. From the philosophers' perspective, the mobile campaign is founded on a paradox every bit as mysterious as mysticism, and far less appealing. It would be easier for Heidegger and Habermas to imagine one hand clapping, than one person communicating – yet that is the core of the mobile concept.

Why Communicate? Saying What you Want

Mobilisation is a coherent approach not only to marketing a device, but to living a life. There are answers to all the big questions about communication which troubled the philosophers. For example, why do people communicate? In the mobile outlook, there can be only one plausible explanation: *The Principle of Want.*

This doesn't mean that people 'want' to communicate. That's one of the strangest things about the mobile vision. On the contrary, people communicate in order to satisfy *other* wants. The mobile is the key to satisfying your wants generally. It gets you things. The result is some extraordinary pictures of a new everyday life:

[The mega-advanced communication device will become] *perhaps as small as a stud in your ear . . . eventually you will simply* **say what you want** *whenever you want it and wherever you want it.* [My emphasis.]

Orange Press Release, 13 July 2000

Here is the key definition: you communicate in order

25

to 'say what you want'. This does not mean what you *mean to say* – it means what you *have to have*.

'Walk down the street, a few blocks away from your favorite Starbucks, pull out your Web-connected cell phone, you get a Starbucks menu, click espresso, and it's sent. And you've not only ordered it, but you've paid and you can go and pick it up.'
New York Times, 2 March 2000

By contrast, Habermas, taking on the spirit of Heidegger, has a different view of the relationship between want and communication. Again, the difference in texture is important – his is such a slow argument, definition by definition. But it is all about saying what you want:

*We even call someone rational if he **makes known a desire or intention**, expresses a feeling or a mood, . . . and **is then able to reassure critics** in regard to the revealed experience by drawing practical consequences from it and behaving consistently thereafter.*[6] [My emphasis.]

For Habermas, you communicate not in order to

satisfy your desire, but crucially in order to *'make known a desire or intention'*. You don't aim to satisfy the want by talking; you aim to disclose it. Then others can respond – that is the suggestion. They can decide, react, help, hinder. To communicate means to make your desires understood, not to pursue their immediate fulfilment.

Now you may say, that's a cumbersome way to think about going to Starbucks. But Habermas doesn't want to take the visit to Starbucks as the epitome of human communication. He wants, on the contrary, to insist that the essential nature of communication is hardly present at all on such occasions or encounters. Habermas's whole philosophy of communication derives from this distinction between pursuing a goal and seeking to communicate. Of course, we use words often to satisfy a want, but for Habermas that isn't true communication. We only actually communicate when we are primarily concerned with making ourselves understood.

In the mobile vision, we have millions of goal-seeking atoms, making basic contacts through the power of the network. In the philosophers' version, you have the slow, distinct 'conversation' through which parties seek a deeper contact . . .

Who Communicates? Device and Voice

We have yet to see, however, just how radical the mobile approach can become. The mobilisation campaign delivers some surprising answers to this basic question: 'Who communicates?'. We have long known from media studies that 'the medium is the message', when it comes to modern communications. But the phone? Here, though, is one answer to 'who communicates?': *Devices*.

*. . . a model to reflect **communications between inanimate objects**, to receive payment for value-added services, as well as charging for conventional voice and data traffic . . .* [My emphasis.]

Orange Press Release, 13 July 2000

Here the company is proposing a new pricing initiative, but as part of that proposition it has to redefine the nature of communication itself, and it does so in this extraordinary way. You might have thought that the meaning of 'inanimate' was precisely 'not able to communicate or be communicated with'. But the language is emphatic, and deliberately reinforces the paradox for rhetorical effect. These are not merely objects, but inanimate objects. Yet they – communications devices and their systems – will be fully recognised as agents of communication. What, then, does the process of communication mean? A touching footnote, for the more traditionally-minded, is provided by the acknowledgement of 'conventional voice' as another possible medium. But even then, 'voice' is subsumed with 'data' and both merge with 'traffic' into the flow of the system itself.

In short, this is a language in which communication has no human agents at all. It is simply a flow of messages, registered in terms of a financial cost. So you check into the system in pursuit of individual desires or aims, and that's the nature of your individual participation. From there, individual agency is swept aside by the sheer flow of traffic through the system.

Another similar plan speaks of:

. . . accelerating the convergence of all communications devices . . .

Orange Press Release, 13 July 2000

As the devices converge, they will be more and more

compatible, better and better able to read one another's messages. Now, clearly, there are all kinds of practical positives – I don't mean to offer a Luddite objection to the technology itself. But I do think it is important to notice what this immensely powerful campaign is doing to the concept of communication – what kind of revolution is being enacted with regard to that fundamental 20th-century idea.

Let's turn back, then, to the old century and see how its philosophers struggled to make their revolution in the concept of communication. Habermas recognised that there are many ways in which a modern society needs to economise on communication. After all, his own theory – like Heidegger's – involves a deep recognition of just how much is involved in authentic human communication. Habermas calls the alternative ways of organising people 'systems'. A system is any way of connecting people up, 'going through' the process of reaching understandings among them, that is, communication. Many human arrangements will have to be made by systems rather than by genuine communication. Some of these systems are as basic as money itself, or bureaucratic procedures, or even sheer power:

*[R]elief mechanisms emerge in the form of **communication media** that either condense or **replace mutual understanding in language**.*[7] [My emphasis.]

No modern society can operate by full-scale dialogue all the time, or even much of the time. You could not run a social security system, or even an education system, like that. All kinds of arrangements get made by substitutes for dialogue – by rules, by the exchange of money or status, by the circulation of impersonal messages. These are 'relief mechanisms', and in a healthy society they would serve to make better spaces in which genuine communication could occur. If communication has to bear the weight of all arrangements, then it will simply collapse under the pressure.

But Habermas foresaw a danger. In the old 20th-century way of such philosophy, he defined that danger as the loss of human texture to parts of our lives: 'The Uncoupling of System and Lifeworld . . .'.[8] By this he meant that the systems would more and more take on a life of their own. The 'lifeworld' is that shared sense of the significance of human actions and experiences, without which the individual is left stranded and searching in isolation for a human meaning to their life. If systems came loose from lifeworlds, then more and more of our lives would be lived according to patterns that had no human significance for us. We would be carrying out tasks without having experiences. And each of us would be living alone. We would feel less and less engaged in our humanity by the institutions and procedures of our society. We would spend our time conforming to rules, rather than engaging in genuine dialogue. And we would find areas of our lives that should depend on dialogue being run as if they were, say, social security systems or bureaucracy. The effect then is that the systems become ever more complicated, as they have to manage more and more of life:

*The more consensus formation in language is relieved by media, the more complex becomes the **network of media-steered interaction**.*[9] [My emphasis.]

As people hand over their lives to be shaped by money or the rules of the power game inside their company or even their family, less and less of life is explored through the dialogue in which one seeks to be understood by others, and to understand them in return. I think most people who were in professions in the late 20th century would be able to make sense of this scenario. Certainly it would be a pretty accurate depiction of life in the British universities of that period, as well as for many working in the health services and other social institutions.

Where once there was communication, now there arise systems:

[A] *heightening of systemic complexity* . . . *unleashes system imperatives that burst the capacity of the lifeworld* . . . [10] [My emphasis.]

This is Habermas's way of saying that we will act increasingly as if we had no freedom to judge, or debate, or even to think. We will feel as if we had no choice. Without communication, there can be no true sense of free choice. The system will drive understanding into the corners of life, and instead substitute procedures to be followed. What counts as reasonable behaviour will then be simply what corresponds to these rules or expectations, these 'imperatives'. Communicative dialogue creates alternatives to explore; systems delete alternatives, and substitute demands.

But the rhetoric of mobilisation would brush aside Habermas's painstaking and heartfelt distinction. The division between system and communication now looks quaint, archaic, a nostalgia for a lost age of leisured inefficiency. What Habermas foresaw as constraint, the mobilisers offer as a liberation. Now the system will do our communication for us.

Just register your desires as swiftly as possible. Then messages will flow to and fro without our needing to engage directly, and that will then be the central meaning of communication. In other words, in the age of full mobilisation, communication would refer primarily to a flow across a system. Voices, and such like, would be simply one small aspect of this traffic. The result, from the perspective of the philosophers, would be the takeover of the term 'communication' by its opposite, the term 'system'.

It's worth returning to Habermas to see just how seriously he might take such a development. He notes already in the latter 20th century 'an extensive uncoupling of system integration and social integration'.[11] 'Integration' is coherence among a group, or even a whole society. Habermas contrasts 'system integration', where people are glued together by common procedures and rules, with 'social integration', where people stay together through a common understanding that they keep working out among themselves. Heidegger too would have understood Habermas's alarm at the rise of 'system integration', whatever their other differences.

In modern life, more and more connections between and among people are made through systems: we are allocated places and times, roles and prospects by means other than dialogue. The university examination process itself is devolving from the old 'viva' tradition to multiple-choice coded assessment programmes. But most importantly, democracy is at stake:

[I]*t is not a matter of indifference to a society whether and to what extent forms of social integration dependent on consensus are repressed and replaced by* **anonymous forms of system-integrative sociation**.[12] [My emphasis.]

The language is cumbersome and makes the argument frustrating to follow. But Habermas isn't being obscure for its own sake. He is trying, perhaps half-successfully, to be precise about a basic distinction between two kinds of social organisation. He is even telling a story in which systems are taking over the role of making people into a 'society' ('sociation'), and communication is being actively 'repressed'. In future, if he is right, people will co-operate because they are each independently following the demands of a system. In a truly communicative society, they would have reached a genuine understanding or 'consensus'. But if you adopted a mobile concept of communication, there would be no difference between system and society, between uniform procedures and genuine consensus.

This is the heart of the matter: is communication simply one function performed by systems, or is it the human pursuit of common understandings? If the mobile concept of communication becomes the norm, that kind of question will feel nostalgic, a remnant of an earlier age. Doesn't it already feel just a little bit quaint, even sentimental?

What is Communicated? Message or Meaning

We have already touched on the next crucial aspect of the mobile redefinition of communication.

There's *who* communicates, and then there's *what* is communicated. Here too, the contrast with the philosophers demonstrates just how radical is the new model. In the rhetoric of mobilisation, dialogue is pushed aside by the term 'exchange'.

It's not a coincidence, I think, that this is more often encountered as a financial term. Of course, we have always talked about 'heated exchanges' and so on, but that's different from taking 'exchange' to be the central description of the process by which people communicate. What, then, is being exchanged? The answer is almost always: a message. Here is an amazing example from the everyday life of a phone executive, as celebrated in the *New York Times*:

[He] *spent most of last Thursday in a meeting . . . 'During that time,' he said, 'I exchanged more than 20 messages with my assistant, who was working in another part of the building, confirming appointments and answering questions.' 'Most of the other participants sent and received messages too . . .'*

New York Times, 14 March 2000

Maybe this is OK as a slightly lurid account of an exceptional person at work, but that's not what is meant. This is the prototype of all our lives, and especially all our working lives!

We will live amidst a tidal flow of messages, coming and going, often registered by our communication 'device' on its own. Here you have the peculiar fusion of opposites that makes the mobile vision of the world. On the one hand, you have the supremely individualistic view, you might almost call it atomistic. There's no real gathering at all. Instead, there are only isolated individuals, each locked in his or her own world, making contact sporadically and for purely functional purposes. On the other hand, there is the system of messages, and at that level there are no human agents at all, because they are overwhelmed by the sheer exuberance of the messages as they multiply and reproduce with a life all of their own. Instead of a group, there is on one level just the individual, and on another level just the pure system, servicing itself as effectively as possible.

The exchange model spreads quickly:

[M]*obile devices will play a paramount role in the future of computing and information exchange ...*
> Nokia Press Release, 28 June 2000

Here we see 'device' replacing 'phone' in an increasingly typical way. The effect is to lay down a grid: communication is exchange and exchange is about information, an aspect of data processing. So the exemplary act of communication is an exchange between devices involving the passing over of information content. Here is an extreme case of 'exchange' communication:

When the shelling and gunfire let up, they send a barrage of scathing insults to Manila's forces by cell phone. . . . 'Texting'? Yes, texting – as in exchanging short typed messages over a cell phone.
                                    New York Times, 5 July 2000

Yes, the article itself is mildly satirical. But what is interesting is the continued use of the word 'exchanging', far more interesting than the highlight on 'texting'. There is of course the phrase 'exchange of fire', and this really extends the exchange model of communication in new ways. 'Now it's personal', says the avenging hero in countless thrillers. Communication would be personalised warfare, and its messages would be – to adapt Hobbes's old saying – nasty, brutish and economical.

The question, then, is: what is happening to certain important words, images and ideas? Something very different from what would have happened under the influence of the philosophers. Habermas in particular provides a graphic contrast with the idea of communication as the exchanging of messages. From his perspective, there are some critical ingredients missing. The most important is 'understanding'. As we have seen, he insists that communication must serve 'the *functions of achieving understanding* in language' [my emphasis].[13] The use of 'in language' in this sentence draws attention to another basic idea about communication. For understanding to be achieved in language, you must have something else in common, and that is meaning. For Habermas, to communicate is to engage with meanings, in the hope of achieving a shared understanding of the world.

Messages are very different from meanings. At most you could say that a message is a very narrowed-down model of meaning – a one-dimensional version of meaning. Habermas's philosophy allows us to distinguish clearly between messages and meaningful expressions:

*And the rationality of those who participate in this communicative practice is determined by whether, if necessary, they could **under suitable circumstances, provide reasons for their expressions.***[14] [My emphasis.]

'Rationality' is Habermas's term for the potentiality which people have to act and speak in ways for which they could give reasons. Expressions, therefore, have meaning insofar as the speaker could give reasons for them. This sounds a bit dry, but reasons needn't be dry: 'I said this because I wanted to convey the feeling of . . . ; the argument for . . . ; the experience of . . . ; to evoke the atmosphere of . . .'. A message is an expression without such reasons, really. It has a purpose rather than reasons. I would send a message to get someone to come to my office at noon. Of course, we need such messages, and they have their place in Habermas's schema. But to make such messages definitive for mainstream communication is to exclude most of the possibilities of human expression. It's a black and white universe.

Habermas makes a sharp division between commands and meaningful communication. Commands have their place. But if a society went down the path of organisation by instruction, it would lose touch with 'good reasons':

*. . . as in relation to imperatives – the **potential for the binding (or bonding) force of good reasons** – a potential which is always contained in linguistic communication – remains unexploited.*[15] [My emphasis.]

For Habermas, a society that arranged its affairs by exchanging 20 or 30 messages an hour (in the background) would soon forget what is involved in a meaningful expression – how much can be said, how much should be said. Such a society would be 'pathological':

Such communication pathologies can be conceived of as a result of a confusion between actions oriented to reaching understanding and actions oriented to success.[16]

In the '30-an-hour' message world, success is the aim. You say as little as possible to make sure you get what you want as fast as you can. Fine in some circumstances. But if a whole society took this as the height of good communication, then it would, in

Habermas's view, lose touch with the deeper sense of communication which has played a fundamental role in human evolution to this point.

When is Communication Going Well? The Right Response

So we come to the question of 'good communication'. Models of communication are never neutral; each implies an ideal scenario. Here the relationship between the 21st-century mobile concept and the 20th-century philosophical concept is strange. They do converge on an idea: *response*. In both approaches, to communicate well means to arouse a response, to which you in turn respond. But the convergence is deceptive, and it hides a deep conflict, perhaps the deepest of all.

In mobile communication, the ideal is represented by the swiftest possible route to the most direct response:

. . . *taking wireless communication beyond two dimensional voice and data into **intelligent, interactive response** to individual customer requests . . .* [My emphasis.]

Orange Press Release, 13 July 2000

43

The key words are culturally rich: 'intelligent', 'interactive'. But this latter is also the give-away. This is a 'virtual reality' model of interactivity. The word 'response' seems to suggest a human element. But, in fact, the ideal scenario has only one human in it. The response comes from the *system itself* and not from another person. Here, then, are the two conflicting aspects of the mobile model brought together. You have the desire-seeking individual making contact with the massive system in order to attain the desired fulfilment. In turn, the system behaves as if it were a fellow human agent, except that it is altogether more efficient and 'intelligent':

Imagine walking into Bloomingdale's and simply saying, 'I'll buy this, thank you,' to which a voice responds, 'That will be $220. Do you confirm?' You then say, 'Yes, I confirm.' The machine says, 'Thank you, have a nice day,' and you walk out the door with your purchase.

New York Times, 2 March 2000

The key phrase is 'a voice responds'. This is the ideal moment. But what a voice, and what response!

Habermas too has 'interaction' and 'response' high on his agenda, but in a different way. Here he really does take the long view, looking right back into the mists of evolution and applying his theories to the behaviour of species like dogs and even simpler organisms! In this theory, communication has evolved from certain very basic interactions where 'response' first occurred:

The interaction is set up in such a way that the beginnings of movement on the part of one organism are the gestures that serve as **the stimulus eliciting a response** *on the part of the other.*[17] [My emphasis.]

Two 'organisms', presumably from the same species, are watching one another. One makes a move, and the second 'responds'. Habermas takes the view that only in the most primitive stages of evolution does the 'response' follow mechanically from the original gesture, without anything resembling 'understanding' coming into play. In other words, 'understanding' begins quite low down on the evolutionary scale, the moment the response involves any kind of processing of the original ges-

45

ture. What gets added by evolution is understanding – first of the other and then of oneself:

*An advantage accrues to participants **who learn not only to interpret the gestures** of others in the light of their own instinctually anchored reactions, **but even to understand the meaning of their own gestures in the light of the expected responses** of others.*[18] [My emphasis.]

Evolution favours those organisms which (or who) respond with insight. Their response follows from a sense of the meaning both of their own gesture and that of the other.

Habermas is clearly talking of pre-verbal gestures: we are in the world of apes, maybe, or even dogs, or perhaps birds on a branch or lizards in the sun. So when you look again at the Bloomingdale's scenario, you get an alarming picture, as if evolution were being thrown backwards, as if under the guise of progress there were an immense degeneration. Meaning is bypassed, as being too slow a medium for the ideal interaction. The aim now is to eliminate understanding altogether, to return to a 'conversation of gestures' more basic even than this early phase that Habermas sketches.

Habermas's evolutionary scheme does not stop there, either. From understanding and responding, we move on to fully rational communication. Now we have the principle of 'communicative rationality': '[B]asing the rationality of an expression on its being **susceptible of criticism** and grounding . . .'.[19] In this phase, it isn't enough to grasp the meaning of what is said. You need to understand the reasons behind it, and its potential weaknesses. At this advanced level, the ideal dialogue looks more like a debate: '[T]he central presupposition of rationality: [expressions] **can be defended against criticism.**'[20] [My emphases.]

Communication is rational only when it has this element of debate, or potential for debate, inside it. Of course, the criticism and defence is usually silent, or implied, or just side-stepped. But it is there in reserve, waiting to be taken up. So you can't claim to understand what someone has said, if you couldn't say why you agree (or disagree): 'We understand a speech act when we know what makes it acceptable.'[21]

From Habermas's point of view, the most disturbing feature of the mobile ideal is that it leaves no space for this criticism at all, and so no scope for achieving true agreement. For you only get a valid agreement on the basis of facing objections or answering questions. In mobile communication, there are no reasons, and no scope for involving them seems to open out. On the contrary: you want what you want, and the voice will comply if you can pay. OK, as an aspect of consumption. But as a model of communication?

You might feel, as I do, that Habermas exaggerates the role of criticism in ideal communication. So you might then turn back to Heidegger for an alternative version of the ideal 'response' with which to assess the mobile scenario. By contrast with the mobile version, Heidegger and Habermas have a lot in common. At the heart is this notion of contact, of response as closeness:

*In the same way, **any answering counter-discourse arises proximally and directly from understanding** what the discourse is about, which is already 'shared' in Being-with.*[22] [My emphasis.]

This has not got Habermas's emphasis on reasons, maybe, but still there is a sense of depth to the connection. There is something *behind* the response. The key is 'understanding', which is the deep-level link between Habermas and Heidegger, a link which is going to mean more and more in the face of the mobile vision.

In the mobile scenario, communication is good when the intelligent response delivers the desired outcome as swiftly as possible. In Heidegger's scenario, communication is good when an answering voice arises not far from the initial utterance, not far in space or time maybe, but more profoundly, *not far* in human understanding. The greater the distance between the answer and the initial voice, the further we are from the ideal. This closeness may not be about agreement. But it is definitely about understanding. Indeed, what Heidegger means by 'understanding' is the closeness of the responding voice to the original. In this argument, 'proximally' means nearby, in touch.

The contrast is really about space and time. For Heidegger, the metaphor is spatial. The answer arises 'close by' the original. For mobilised communication, the ideal is expressed in terms of time, and the response comes as swiftly as possible after the request, for that is what the first voice utters in this scenario. Habermas keeps Heidegger's ideal of closeness, but he adds more sense of argumentativeness, of difference. Either way, the philosophers' ideal scenario feels slow and even tentative. The answering voice takes its time, feels the way.

For both the mobile campaign and the philosophers, a lot of what passes for ordinary communication is less than ideal, even inadequate. In mobile terms, the responses are often too slow, and perhaps the requests aren't clear enough. In philosophical terms, the responses are too fast, and there isn't enough time given to achieving understanding. Here is the real crunch. Both schools (let's call them that) regard ordinary communication as imperfect, or, more positively, as having the potential to be improved. Mobilisation seeks to improve ordinary communication by giving it new channels, clarifying the real meaning of the message, speeding up the response time, whereas the philosophers want communication to be more gradual, more weighted by the search for understanding. Heidegger gives a twist by adding: 'Only he who already understands can listen.'[23] There is a closeness even before true listening. In other words, most of the time, people are not really listening to one another. Again, there is such a sense of slow closing in, or the difficult process of making true contact.

You could say that both mobile campaign and philosophers are revolutionary in their approach to communication. Both regard normal, accepted communication as inadequate, as not living up to its own potential. So you could see these as rival utopian approaches to communication: competing ideals. Knowledge has much to do with both utopias, for the value of communication is everywhere linked to the value of knowledge.

What Do You Learn From Communication? Information and Understanding

It is often said that we are entering 'the information age'. Until recently, the epitome or symbol of the information age has been the Internet, as an aspect of 'computers'. But now the phone is poised to take over and include the Internet within its empire of communication. It may be that the most influential aspect of mobilisation is going to turn out to be this redefining of the information age, and thus of the future which our society is trying to imagine itself as beginning upon. Here is a key example (with a negative twist in the tail):

[A]s more phones become programmable and **capable of communicating with the Internet and downloading information**, there will be more opportunities for computer viruses . . . [My emphasis.]

New York Times, 8 June 2000

This 'communicating' means making a connection, entering into the network. Again, it is the device which is 'capable of communicating', in the new language. The 'other' in the communication is a network, not an agent. Of course, many good things can happen – and I'm quite as likely to use it as anyone else. But that's the point. These good things are going to lend credibility to the language of the campaign which surrounds the mobile phone. It is by no means necessary for the technology and its advantages to be wrapped up in this particular model of communication. There are all sorts of alternatives that one can easily imagine – indeed, you only have to compare the way in which the Internet itself emerged and developed with the ways in which the mobile is now being presented.

If the mobile of the future were not such a genuinely powerful and appealing tool, none of this would really matter. But because the mobile is going to be so important, the way in which ideas are associated with it is also important. As society adopts this technology, it is inevitably going to diffuse the associated ideas, images and ways of thinking. At the moment, those ways of thinking centre on the redefining of communication as a potentiality of the device itself – and with that goes a redefinition of knowledge as 'information', because that is what can be imagined flowing into the device as it communicates. In other words, the potential tragedy is that this most rich of technological developments is being packaged in such an impoverishing vision. And this in turn matters because there are a number of other powerful developments with which it fits – in education, in a view of work and of democracy itself.

Learning is being redefined as part of this new model of communication. To learn now means to have the right information pushed at you as efficiently as possible, and education or training will then fit into the wider vision in which:

[U]*sers can access personal Web pages and configure the services they will get through the phone:* **specific information 'pushed' to them** *at a given time . . .*

New York Times, 14 March 2000

*'Our ultimate aim . . . is for anyone, anywhere, any-time to **get access to highly personalized informa-tion** direct from Reuters.'*

New York Times, 12 January 2000

[My emphases.]

Learning, in this scenario, is a process of making sure the right information comes your way as quickly as possible. So communication comes into play as the process by which this information is posted to the right address and delivered with the least possible delay. Ideally, information would be sent out like a FedEx cargo, under guarantee from the agency, whether school or university, writer or publisher, television channel or newspaper.

The old philosophy of the last century provides the basis for an alternative view of knowledge and communication. Perhaps, more pessimistically, you could say that the old philosophy tells us what will be lost in the redefinition of education and know-ledge. Habermas concentrates most on this ques-tion, as part of his wider concern with rationality – with the potential which human beings have for doings things in ways for which they can provide good reasons:

[F]or *rationality has less to do with the possession of knowledge than with **how speaking and acting subjects acquire and use knowledge** . . .*[24] [My emphasis.]

You could not get a stronger contrast with the model in which information is 'pushed' in a correctly targeted way. Instead, you have the idea of a process in which people actively search for knowledge, as part of the wider process of understanding one another. In the mobile scenario, the more information you acquire, the more efficiently you are learning. But Habermas is concerned with 'how' people gain knowledge and 'how' they use it. In his theory, two people could have gained the same information, but one might have acquired it in far richer and more enabling ways than the other. Specifically, a person who had gained knowledge through genuine dialogue might have a richer understanding than someone who had just got hold of the data as swiftly as possible.

Again, you can see the contrast in terms of rival utopian visions. The mobile utopian vision is about instant access to exactly the right information to suit your immediate needs. It is all about gaining, acquiring as efficiently as possible. By contrast, the philosopher lingers over the process of acquisition, precisely the stage which is minimised by the mobile. Put it this way: Habermas would not see acquiring the maximum information in the minimum time as a good definition of learning. But it is the definition implied by the mobile rhetoric of data-pushing and swift access.

The contrast with Habermas is the more significant because the mobile model fits so conveniently with influential approaches in education, in politics and in the media. We are, for instance, employing assessment schemes which subject teachers to judgement resembling the mobile model, rather than the philosophical alternative. A mobile university would look very different from one based on 'communicative rationality'. A company which trained its staff by pushing information out to them would feel very different from one which kept space for at least some mutual understanding. A state which addressed its citizens on the mobile model would stage very different elections from one which tried to keep open spaces for criticism and new consensus. It seems only too plausible that our election campaigns will involve the more and more accurate 'targeting' of 'information'; that we are entering the era of 'm-politics' and leaving behind the ideal, at least, of a more communicative style of political life.

Turn still further back to Heidegger, and again you can see the roots of what Habermas has been saying, and also get an even stronger contrast with the mobilised view of knowledge. For Heidegger, communication was part of a wider phenomenon which he called 'discourse'. Communication was discourse expressing itself. Discourse itself seemed rather mysterious in that pronouncement. Here we can see that, for Heidegger, discourse is about a kind of knowledge: 'Discourse is the Articulation of Intelligibility.'[25] Discourse is any way in which people give expression to their sense that the world is understandable, that a certain experience of the world can make sense.

For Heidegger, communication is the process by which people share, and encourage, their sense that the world can be comprehended, that their experience can become significant. Without such communication, therefore, people will lose confidence in the possibility of understanding their experience of the world. A person who cannot communicate will also find the world more opaque. A society that does not communicate will not give its members the chance to feel that their experience adds up to any kind of coherent whole. Education, then, in this view would be all about supporting the feeling of 'intelligibility' by opening out lines of communication.

Not that Heidegger ignored information in his approach to either knowledge or communication. Here is his rather elaborate idea:

*'Communication' in which one makes assertions – **giving information, for instance** – is a special case of that communication which is grasped in principle existentially. In this more general kind of communication, the Articulation of Being with another is understandingly constituted.*[26] [My emphasis.]

What does he mean? In the present context, he means that giving and receiving information should only be taken as a small aspect of the wider process of communication, and wider field of understanding. In Heidegger's terms, the mobile model threatens to make a minor part of communication into the central case. Of course, information is passed across. But that is as part of the wider process in which people seek to share their sense of being.

I suppose, on the whole, the postmodern encounter of the new mobile culture and the old philosophy of communication points towards some pessimistic conclusions. Heidegger and Habermas certainly draw attention to the losses which might be the underside of 21st-century progress. But there is also a hint of an alternative, truly utopian conclusion. The mobile technology is clearly not going to be switched off. It is going to develop in all kinds of new directions. But does that technology need to come packaged in the mobile concept of communication? Could we have the mobile without the mobilisation? Might we, for instance, connect the new technologies of 'information' with the older models of 'how speaking and acting subjects acquire knowledge'? In this utopian glimpse, you might have the mobile technology combined with a richer and more humane sense of what it means to communicate and to learn through communication.

What's the Future of Communication? Value or Money

But that utopian outcome doesn't look likely . . . On the contrary, mobilisation, the whole promotional atmosphere, is turning the mobile technology into a symbol of a certain very narrow vision of modernisation. The mobile is the symbol of the future at the start of the new millennium. And in that symbol, money takes over many areas that in the 20th century had held out against it.

The mobile has, of course, a down-to-earth financial pitch, like any other product being sold:

[A] *simple means of communication that makes financial sense ...*

'The Orange Way', www.orange.co.uk,
18 July 2000

But even here there is a hint of the deeper significance. Communication is being increasingly measured in terms of money, becoming 'metered'. Of course, some communication always has been done with the meter running. But now metering is going to be a very direct part of everyday contact all the time, at work and beyond. How many resources have been sunk into this five-minute discussion? How much was arranged? How much skill was acquired? How many customers were appeased? The question is whether there will remain, anywhere, a space for communication which does not make financial sense, or is not analogous to financial sense. Will the only test of communication be: how much did it cost?

The prospects are not good for those with a lingering attachment to the old models of dialogue. We are, in the language of mobilisation, only at the beginning of the new era. This object, once a phone and increasingly a 'device', looks set to carry into the 21st century the idea that communication is a sub-set of exchange, and, as such, it will ultimately fall under the rule of money:

For those still fixated with e-commerce, forget it . . . The latest thing is m-commerce, as in mobile phone.
www.guardianunlimited, 4 July 2000

This is a moment really worth pausing over. The meaning of 'mobile' is changing here with the introduction of the 'm' in 'm-commerce'. Now the same 'm' will stand for mobile and for money. Ultimately it is money which is destined to be mobilised in the coming century. It may turn out that the mobilisation of talk, of communication, of information, is only a stage on the way to the bigger mobilisation.

The speeding up of exchange is going to be the ruling metaphor in the world of finance, making a:

*Promise to turn your cell phone or handheld organizer into **an electronic wallet**.* [My emphasis.]
New York Times, 2 March 2000

There is a sense of magic, transfiguration, meta-morphosis. Objects seem to be on the verge of leading a life of their own. New categories are being born. What will it mean when one object is both your communication device, your organiser and your money supplier? This m-device heralds a new dance. A new conception of everyday life is being sketched, and at the heart of this new conception is the new concept of communication. The mobilising of communication turns out to be the precursor, the necessary precondition, for this larger mobilisation of the everyday. This 'm' stands for a new order of everyday life: faster, neater, sharper.

From the old philosophy, we get a different perspective on a similar future. First, from Habermas, there is the idea that changes in communication will go with a new society. But here the process is seen as ambiguous and often destructive:

*The transfer of action co-ordination **from language over to steering media . . . such as money and power** . . .* [These media] *encode a purposive-rational attitude . . .*[27] [My emphasis.]

And Habermas had not glimpsed the m-commerce world! This m-future goes much further than the 'transfer' he is imagining. Now we are looking, in the terms of his philosophy, towards a future where communication is incorporated into 'money and power' so thoroughly that it has no separate sphere at all. There will, if the m- is the future, be no idea of communication distinct from the idea of commerce. To communicate will mean the same thing as to exchange money. The two activities will simply be merged.

But for Habermas that merger, or take-over, would be a disaster, and an irreversible one. It is only because the idea of communication remains partly distinct from power and money that there is any place from which to criticise those systems. The mobile here begins to signify the end of philosophy itself, as understood by the tradition running (with many strains and breaks) from Heidegger to Habermas. Their ideas would be swept aside by this

new *m-communication*, which would be imperme-
able to their thinking.

Communication would then become a matter of
pure technique. But just think how many places
there are where you are offered just such a model of
communication! How many opportunities you
have, at work, or in your personal life, to acquire
better communication skills, as if that were quite
independent of any content that you might have to
communicate, or anyone you might wish to speak
with. If m-communication overcomes communicative action and communication rationality, it will be
the end of what this philosophy calls 'the lifeworld'
– that is, the world experienced as a lived environment: my world, our world, endowed with my and
our meanings, lived from within, layered with our
interpretations. We have no sense of identity outside
such a world, not personal identity. But there are
alternatives to deep identity – most notably lifestyle
– and m-communication goes with the triumph of
lifestyle over lifeworld.[28]

It may even be the destiny of the mobile to bring
about the cultural disaster which Habermas has
foreseen, however clumsily he has expressed the
vision:

*Societal **subsystems** differentiated out via media of this kind can make themselves **independent of the lifeworld**, which gets shunted aside into the system environment.*[29] [My emphasis.]

The mobile would be the supreme medium for turning everything around into a system, driving out the process of reaching understanding, replacing meanings with messages, consensus with instructions and insight with information. In that process, the lifeworld would be 'shunted aside'. We would be left, co-ordinated but not connected, in a shared web of systems for working and consuming, learning and being together. At last there would be 'a technicization of the lifeworld'.

The terminology is unhappy, almost an example of what it is protesting against: the loss of spontaneous understanding. But in his way, Habermas is imagining a world which cannot distinguish between a credit card transaction and a conversation – or a world where the ideal conversation aspires to the condition of a credit card transaction. That would also be a world in which your diary is your wallet: at last your money and your life will be properly interchangeable! Having too many messages to deal with, we will have to settle for a good lifestyle instead of the good life to which philosophers have pointed since classical times.

To adapt Habermas, you could say that the big question is: how much of the world is to lie outside the lifeworld? If the lifeworld is the space in which we give our own significance to experience, not as isolated individuals, but in coherent dialogue with others, then there's a strong argument for saying that, for each person, the lifeworld is shrinking. More and more of our life will be lived in a systems space, where efficient and minimal messaging will replace the slow and messy process of dialogue. Two different kinds of example occur to me: one public and one personal.

The public example is from the news, and takes us back to those truckers with their mobile phone revolution whom we met at the start. You could also use your mobile to consult the government's list of closed petrol stations in September 2000. But at the heart of this conflict – and no doubt the others which will take its place before you read this book – is a wall of silence: there is not even the hint of contact between the actual protagonists. Messages are good at setting up the confrontation more quickly and keeping us informed. You can even use your mobile to e-mail (or m-mail) your views to the BBC. In *Middlemarch*, George Eliot wrote of 'the roar that lies on the other side of silence'. Here, perhaps, is the silence that lies on the other side of the roar of messages. Maybe it would still be good to talk, sometimes, even though it is often great to communicate so swiftly. But it seems that no one can risk the messiness of the open-ended dialogue: how can anyone begin talking with *such people* as the other side? Only a swift message in the ear – or on the screen – can 'resolve' this dispute! Yet mysteriously, disputes refuse to vaporise. On the same day as the petrol crisis reaches a climax, there is a report of a mortar attack in Belfast. Surely the time for talking *must* be past? Haven't those people 'got the message' *yet*?

The personal example concerns changes in what the philosopher Jacques Derrida has called 'the university space'. When I finish a course now, I hand out a form to students to get 'feedback'. It sounds good, a democratic process. But then just look at the form. There is a list of bullet points, and boxes to tick. Were you interested: Yes/No, or maybe 1–5? Was it audible? Did it fit the course handbook? And the forms are carefully anonymous, so that there can be no retribution or, presumably, corruption. The result is a tide of numbers: one's interest index is only 2.7 this year for Literary History, though one scored 3.6 for audibility in Modern Tragedy. This stuff might be alright if it were the prelude to a dialogue, but as ever in the fast world of mobilised opinion, this is the substitute for dialogue. The feedback form is born of despair, in its little way, despair at the possibility of ever undertaking actual contact with so many people, and across such absolute divisions of self-interest as must separate the student who is being assessed and the teacher who will do the grading. This too is a roar with a deep silence on the other side.

Ultimately, it is the future which is the subject of this 'Postmodern Encounter', the future as conceived in terms of communication. At times, the mobile promotion hypes the future like any other advertising, promising:

> ... *a range of services to take wireless communications into a new dimension* ...
>
> www.orange.co.uk, 18 July 2000

But at other times, the rhetoric of mobilisation

seems to go beyond advertising hype, and intervene in the theory of modern utopias, most notably in such moments as we saw at the beginning:

Today, wireless phones provide more than 94 million, or one in every three people in the US, with the freedom to communicate – whenever they want, wherever they want.

Nokia Press Release, 12 July 2000

That old-fashioned word 'wireless' – which in Britain used to mean the *radio* – has been reborn as the symbol of a new utopian dream of a wireless world, where 'freedom' will mean the power to communicate on your own terms, 'whenever' and 'wherever' *you* choose. It is a powerful vision of the m-future. In this encounter, this m-future has been defining itself in a dialogue with Heidegger, Habermas and the philosophy of authentic communication, from 'talk' and 'discourse' to 'communicative action'. That philosophy of communication is no more finished than the mobile campaign. Will the old philosophy find new alternatives to the m-future? Let's hope we will recover a touch of 's-communication', where 's' stands for 'still'.

Appendix: Brief Background to Heidegger and Habermas

Martin Heidegger
Introduction

Martin Heidegger (1889–1976) was the most important, and also the most controversial, influence on modern European philosophy – often referred to as the 'continental' tradition by contrast with the 'analytic' approach of the Anglo-American school. Heidegger's major work was *Being and Time*, published in 1927. There he gave expression to a philosophical vision of 'man' as a being 'thrown' into the world, and always in search of an 'authentic' identity. Though Heidegger himself soon drew close to German Fascism in the 1930s, these ideas from *Being and Time* reached far wider than his own particular approach, and influenced thinkers from all political, moral and religious quarters throughout the 20th century. Other major developments of Heidegger's thinking are found in 'What is Metaphysics?' (1929) and *Letter on Humanism* (1947).

Being and Time

This 'Postmodern Encounter' draws upon *Being and Time* for Heidegger's views of talk and communica-

70

tion. In that book, Heidegger saw himself as recalling philosophy to 'the question of Being', and developed a complex account of our 'being-in-the-world'. Heidegger believed that Western philosophy had lost touch with the important questions of human existence. Writing in the aftermath of the First World War, he gave an urgent account of human life as a search for its own meaning and identity, unaided by any external authority or fixed values.

Heidegger's treatment of 'talk' and 'discourse' arises as part of his picture of the human search for the significance of our own 'being':

Discoursing or talking is the way in which we articulate 'significantly' the intelligibility of being-in-the-world.[30]

Discourse is broader than talk, including all of our inner and outer expression which plays the same role as talking. No single concept has been more important to modern thought than this idea of discourse.

Talk and Discourse
- Do NOT have the purpose of transmitting messages or information.
- Are NOT ways of getting things we want more efficiently.

- Do NOT give expression to 'me–I'.

- DO have the purpose of finding significance.
- DO have the purpose of sharing understanding.
- DO give expression to human being-in-the-world.

These ideas of communication were taken up by important thinkers, including Karl Jaspers (1883–1969), who in *Philosophy* (1932) argued that only in 'communication' could man 'become himself'. While Heidegger drew closer to the Nazis, Jaspers courageously refused all collaboration and continued to uphold this communicative ideal, which, however, still had deep roots in Heidegger's original ideas of discourse and talk.

Jürgen Habermas
Introduction

Jürgen Habermas has been a leading influence on contemporary thought since the appearance of his monumental two-volume *Theory of Communicative Action* (1981). There, Habermas sees himself as laying 'The Foundations of Social Science in the Theory of Communication'.[31] The direct influences on this theory are sociological theorists, notably Max Weber and Theodor Adorno. Habermas belongs to the tradition of the democratic Left, and has been a notable critic of the inheritances of Fascism in Germany and beyond. But in its core vision, Habermas's work also develops Heidegger's story in which talk has arisen to give expression to the human search for meaning, rather than to convey useful messages. Habermas acknowledges his critical involvement with Heidegger's thought in *The Philosophical Discourse of Modernity* (1987), in which he presents himself as discovering a lost opportunity which his predecessor had overlooked in his own system. The later developments of Habermas's arguments are gathered in his collection entitled *Between Facts and Norms* (1996), in which there is an increasing engagement with the ethical and legal implications of his ideas of communicative action.

The Theory of Communicative Action

Habermas starts with the question: what does it mean to say that a person, or an action, or a way of life, is *rational*? His ultimate aim is to give an account of the evolution of modern society in terms of different ways of being rational, or of becoming *more* rational. For Habermas, to become more modern means to become more rational, which sounds rather optimistic or even complacent. However, he makes a vital distinction between two different ways of being rational. First there is 'instrumental rationality', which is about 'successful self-maintenance' – that is, the effective pursuit of your own interests, the efficient pursuit of your own goals.[32] Then, by contrast, there is 'communicative rationality'.

Communicative Rationality

- Is NOT defined as the competitive pursuit of your own aims and interests.
- Is NOT about devising 'strategies' for success.

- IS about the achievement of shared understandings through language and other means of communication.
- IS about being open to criticism and able to give *good reasons* for your beliefs, decisions and actions.

'Communicative action' is based upon this kind of rational agreement, achieved either though actual dialogue or through other means of achieving shared understanding.

In Habermas's theory, communicative rationality has the 'potential' to create a society which is more modern in the sense of being more open. But he sees the rival, instrumental rationality as being in the ascendant, creating a society which is more modern only in the sense of being more effective at delivering the goals of those in power, or more efficient at servicing the systems of money. Habermas has produced a new way of criticising modern society, in which many values and ideas associated with the political and intellectual Left are combined with an idea of communication that still has deep roots in Heidegger.

Notes

1. *Being and Time*, p. 208.
2. *Basic Philosophical Writings*, p. 76 (*Philosophy*).
3. *Being and Time*, p. 312.
4. *Theory of Communicative Action I*, p. 287
5. Ibid., pp. 286–8.
6. Ibid., p. 15.
7. *Theory of Communicative Action II*, p. 181.
8. Ibid., p. 153.
9. Ibid., p. 184.
10. Ibid., p. 155.
11. Ibid., p. 185.
12. Ibid., p. 186.
13. *Theory of Communicative Action I*, p. 308.
14. Ibid., p. 17.
15. Ibid., p. 305.
16. Ibid., p. 332.
17. *Theory of Communicative Action II*, p. 7.
18. Ibid., p. 12.
19. *Theory of Communicative Action I*, p. 9.
20. Ibid., p. 16.
21. Ibid., p. 297.
22. *Being and Time*, p. 207.
23. Ibid., p. 208.
24. *Theory of Communicative Action I*, p. 8.

25. *Being and Time*, p. 204.

26. Ibid., p. 205.

27. *Theory of Communicative Action II*, p. 183.

28. For the rise of 'lifestyle', see e.g. Anthony Giddens, *Modernity and Self-Identity* (Cambridge: Polity Press, 1991).

29. *Theory of Communicative Action II*, p. 183.

30. *Being and Time*, p. 204.

31. *Theory of Communicative Action II*, p. 3.

32. *Theory of Communicative Action I*, p. 171.

Further Reading

The key texts have been used in the following editions:

Martin Heidegger, *Being and Time*, trans. J. Macquarrie and E. Robinson (Oxford: Blackwell, 1962). For further reading, I recommend: Part V, Sections 31 ('Being-There as Understanding'), 34 ('Being-There and Discourse') and 35 ('Idle Talk').

Jürgen Habermas, *The Theory of Communicative Action I*, trans. T. McCarthy (London: Heinemann, 1984).

Jürgen Habermas, *The Theory of Communicative Action II*, trans. T. McCarthy (Cambridge: Polity, 1984).

The most useful background sources are:

C. Guignon (ed.), *The Cambridge Companion to Heidegger* (Cambridge, UK: Cambridge University Press, 1993).

S.K. White (ed.), *The Cambridge Companion to Habermas* (Cambridge, UK: Cambridge University Press, 1995).

I have also cited:

Karl Jaspers, *Basic Philosophical Writings*, trans. E.

Ehrlich, L. Ehrlich and G. Pepper (Humanities Press, 1994).

Other related works include:

Avital Ronell, *The Telephone Book: Technology, Schizophrenia, Electric Speech* (Lincoln: University of Nebraska Press, 1989). This is a deconstructive reflection on Heidegger's theory of conscience as a 'call', using excerpts from his involvement with the Nazi Party as a counterpoint.

Geoff Mulgan, *Connexity: How to Live in a Connected World* (London: Chatto, 1997). A balanced response to the social impacts of new communications.

James Gleick, *Faster* (London: Abacus, 1999). A chronicle of contemporary relationships between new technology and human experience.

Dedication

For Yvonne, with love – staying in touch as ever.